MICHAEL AYRTON
(London 1921 - 1975 London)

MICHAEL AYRTON

R.S. JOHNSON INTERNATIONAL/645 NORTH MICHIGAN AVENUE

CHICAGO, ILLINOIS 60611/TELEPHONE (312) 943-1661

HOMAGE TO
Michael Ayrton

1921 - 1975

FEBRUARY 1984

Library of Congress Catalog Card Nº 83-083162

On Cover
38. **Mirror Maze** (bronze, copper and perspex), 1966.

8. **Demeter Head** (black ink wash drawing), 1965.

MICHAEL AYRTON (1921-1975)

November 16, 1983 marked the eighth anniversary of the death of Michael Ayrton. Perhaps for the first time it is possible to distance ourselves sufficiently from Ayrton's volcanic and complex artistic personality and to consider his accomplishments with a relatively objective eye.

Going back to 1944, Michael Ayrton, then twenty-three years old, took over John Piper's post as art critic for **The Spectator** in London and later did criticism on BBC. At the same time that he continually drew and painted, Ayrton's activities branched out into film-making, theatrical design, book illustrations and finally the writing of novels. His lists of accomplishments in any of these fields are formidable. Until recently, these accomplishments have tended to cloud over Ayrton's primary achievement, that in sculpture, a domain to which the artist consecrated the greater part of his energies over the last twenty-five years of his life.

* * *

In the 1940's, the gradual rejection of painterly qualities and the increasing emphasis on sculptural forms were the key elements in the artistic development of Michael Ayrton. In June of 1949, at an exhibition organized by the Wakefield City Art Gallery, Ayrton stated :

> «...The work of sculptors was the most potent single influence on painting during the formative years of the Renaissance ; Giotto owed much to the Pisani, Masaccio, much to Donatello, and Leonardo's master was Verrocchio. Sculptural form realised pictorially by drawing was at the centre of the Renaissance and is the significant factor in the 19th Century art of Ingres, Degas and Seurat and in the

5

20th Century art of Juan Gris and Wyndham Lewis. It is also the chief virtue of the Cubists. Herein my main interest lies. I would go further and maintain that this astringent form of art is needed today to balance the powerful influence which Impressionism, Expressionism, Neo-Impressionism and so on still combine to exercise upon contemporary painting.»[1]

Michael Ayrton's first specific move toward sculpture could be dated to 1950 and his lengthy visits to the Paris studio of the Swiss sculptor Alberto Giacometti. However, the basis of this interest really goes back further, to student days in Vienna where Ayrton spent months copying drawings, particularly those of Albrecht Durer, in the Albertina Museum. From this early period and until the end of his life, Ayrton drew daily :

«Drawing is the centre. To me, drawing is not only the central activity from which both painting and sculpture stem but the core of visual experience. In the act of drawing one discovers what one is doing. That drawing is, in itself, an act of discovery means to me that the most profound experience transmitted to the spectator through drawing is the same revelation as the artist has made to himself and not necessarily something which he specifically wished to communicate to someone else.»[2]

It was a combination of his addiction to drawing and the gradual realisation of the limitations of drawing which led Michael Ayrton to three-dimensional sculpture. The artist summed up these ideas in 1959 :

«There are times when one's drawings, coming out from the paper, insist on becoming sculpture, at the next stage, rather than painting. Over this one has no control, unless one deliberately ignores the dictates of one's vision...»[3].

In the early 1950's, Michael Ayrton's sculpture owed much in its technical development to Henry Moore (the two artists eventually also collaborated on a complete works catalog of Giovanni Pisano)[4]. Moore showed Ayrton how to work directly in plaster on iron armatures ; he also showed Ayrton how the properties of wax could be useful in small models. Finally it was Moore who proposed the use of bones as a sculptural medium. Ayrton became intrigued with the possibilities in the use of bones and bone forms in sculpture :

«The bone is so directly relevant to function, so absolute in shape, that it is in itself transcendental sculpture. A bone invites metamorphosis and recreates itself in the process. The skeleton of a bird can become the bare trees of a mysterious landscape and the skull of a rabbit or the breastbone of a goose will show you how it can become a helmet or wings or a fish...»[5].

Ayrton's sculptures often combined bones and human figures through which the artist created a most powerful imagery. It was chiefly through these combinations that Ayrton also reflected on the concept of time and the ambiguities of time which ideas were to become so basic to much of Ayrton's painting, drawing and sculpture.

*   *   *

The early sculptures of Michael Ayrton were concerned with a multitude of themes : time, figures and stress, the parallels of human and animal forms and others. Gradually however most of Ayrton's sculpture came to revolve around one myth of antiquity : that of Daedalus and Icarus. This general theme moved to the center of Ayrton's ideas in the middle of 1950's, at the same time that the artist's intellectual interests turned from northern Italy and the Renaissance to an intense preoccupation with the ancient world of southern Italy. This new direction was established most clearly after Ayrton's visit in May 1956 to the ruins of the earliest Greek colony in Italy, Cumae near the bay of Naples. Michael Ayrton recalled that visit :

«It was not Virgil's epic, it was Berlioz's setting of it that rang in my ears when I first entered the Acropolis of Cumae to find myself in thrall to a Greek myth which ends in Italy. It was at Cumae that Aeneas first landed in Italy. But it was quite a different myth that had brought me there. The myth with which I came to be concerned and which indeed inspired almost all my work for upwards of thirteen years was that of Daedalus, the archetypal craftsman who built the labyrinth on Crete, to house the Minotaur, and was himself imprisoned in it with his son Icarus. In the labyrinth he made wings for himself and his son and they became the first men to fly. At the end of that flight, during which Icarus died in contest with Apollo, it was at Cumae that Daedalus landed.»[6]

The simplest description of this myth would have Icarus, in the flight from Crete, flying too close to the sun which melted the wax attaching his wings. Icarus then fell to drown in the Aegean Sea. Instead of this version of the story, Ayrton interpreted the tragedy of Icarus as the result of a sexual attack on the God Apollo, which attack obviously was lost by Icarus[7].

In 1960-1962, Ayrton presented these ideas in a series of bronzes and then in another series in 1963-1965. As these bronzes developed, Ayrton's Daedalus, the man of action in the myth, took on a greater and greater significance. As the legend was told, the story had commenced on Crete in the palace of King Minos at Knossos. It had been there that Daedalus, working for the King, had built a Maze to confine a Minotaur conceived by Minos'wife Pasiphae who had been impregnated by a bull sent from the sea by Poseidon. Daedalus, for having assisted Poseidon, had been imprisoned, together with his son Icarus, in the same Maze as the Minotaur. After flying out of the Maze and after having lost his son Icarus, Daedalus flew on to Cumae where he was forced by the Gods to construct a temple in honor of Apollo. Later in Sicily, Daedalus was obliged to construct still another maze. In fact, Daedalus' life revolved around the construction of one maze after another.

«You will build a labyrinth. That is the central purpose of your life. Master of many crafts you may be, but finally you will discover that all your life you have been a maze maker»[8].

*   *   *

Michael Ayrton's earliest «maze» sculptures referred to the prototypes of the myth. Gradually these concepts evolved into a concern with the reactions of man to a Maze, which Ayrton extended to signify man's entire environment with its constant stress of confinement and needs for release. From physical stress, Ayrton's drawings and sculpture turned eventually to the problems of mental stress and the idea of each man finding himself in his own maze which he himself has constructed around and within himself.

A central figure in the Daedalus/Icarus legend was the Minotaur. Half man and half bull, the Minotaur in antiquity was considered to be a wild monster who loved to gorge on live bodies of boys and girls sent to him in tribute by the Athenians. In more modern times, the Minotaur became a symbol of male potency with which a Picasso, for example, attempted to identify himself. For Michael Ayrton, the Minotaur was an almost human being whose tragedy became more acute as it became more human, whose suffering increased as its desires and sensitivity were rejected because of being found in an ugly, uncontrolled and uncivilized body. Ayrton describes the Minotaur :

What is a man that I am not a man sitting cramped pupate in this chrysalis ?
My tongue is gagged with cud and lolls around words
To speak impeded of my legend death.

My horns lack weapon purpose, cannot kill
And cannot stab the curtain of the dark.

* * *

The theme of Daedalus. Icarus and the Minotaur found a further development in 1968-1969 in Ayrton's so-called Arkville Maze, commissioned by New York financier Armand G. Erpf. Constructed in the Catskills in upstate New York, this modern maze is a vast sculpture of brick, stone and bronze and has 1,680 feet of intricate passageways, with eight foot walls in which were used 210,000 bricks. With a 200 foot diameter, this would appear to be the largest maze (or labyrinth) constructed since antiquity. Within this maze are two main chambers, one with a large bronze **Minotaur** and the other with an equally large **Daedalus/Icarus Matrix**. This latter area contains one technical innovation in the form of bronze mirrors lining the chamber. Ayrton's mental perception of the maze was more far-reaching however than this physical description :

> «The labyrinth is at once ambiguous in its form and in its nature. To Daedalus, its walls were dense and impenetrable, translucent and illusory. It may also be as implacable as stone or as impalpable as smoke...»[9].

* * *

The technical innovation of the bronze mirrors in the Arkville Maze made its first appearance in Ayrton's sculpture in **Mirror Maze** of 1966. In this latter bronze, a crouching Daedalus-like figure is surrounded on five sides with bronze mirrors which reflect the figure towards the observer, looking in from the sixth side-opening of the chamber.

Another technical innovation appeared in Ayrton's bronzes in 1969 with the artist's discovery of the use of a glass-like material called perspex which reflects light with the same degree of intensity with which it transmits light. In Ayrton's words :

> «In 1969 a small piece of neutral perspex, a substance at once dense and translucent yet with the power to reflect, extended my means to give physical expression to metaphorical forms as to the idea of what lies within or beyond the mirror. The idea itself is not new, except perhaps in sculpture. Lewis Carroll took Alice through the looking-glass and Jean Cocteau conceived, on film, the means to take Orpheus through the mirror and into the nether world...»[10].

Making use of perspex, Michael Ayrton, in the last six years of his life, developed a series of «reflector bronzes». In their simplest form, these works show a bronze, backed with a sheet of perspex reflecting the figure and suggesting the presence of another identical figure on the other side. In a more complex development, Ayrton actually placed another figure on the other side of the perspex so that an observer the would be presented with three images : that of the original bronze : that of the reflection of that bronze ; and finally that of the second bronze seen hazily through the perspex. Placing these works on the turnstyles already used in many of his earlier bronzes, Ayrton achieved an even more complex dynamic relationship among the various images in that the figures, seen directly and indirectly, simultaneously reflected and transmitted, are found to be both penetrating into and emerging out of their respective mazes.

This latter concept is basic to the principle theme of Ayrton's later sculpture : that of man building a maze around and within himself. In his novel **The Maze Maker**, Ayrton has Daedalus state :

> «All this long burrowing and building, to protect or to imprison, this flight through the sky and tunnelling in the earth, seems to me now to add up to no more than the parts of a single great maze which is my life. This maze for the Maze Maker I made

9. **Mazemaker** (white chalk on black paper), 1965.

from experience and from circumstance. Its shape identifies me. It has been my goal and my sanctuary, my journey and its destination. In it I have lived continually, ceaselessly enlarging it and turning it to and fro from ambition, hope and fear. Toy, trial and torment, the topology of my labyrinth remains ambiguous. Its materials are at once dense, impenetrable, translucent and illusory. Such a total maze each man makes round himself and each is different from every other, for each contains the length, breadth, height and depth of his own life»[11].

*   *   *

Michael Ayrton is one of Great Britain's most significant post-war sculptors. One of the distinguishing marks of his sculpture is its constant reference to the artist's own past innovations which in turn became integrated and re-integrated into newly developing conceptions. The result, as we are now able to judge, is an astounding unity of the whole of the artist's twenty-five years of creativity in sculpture.

Ayrton's sculptures are highly complex : they cannot be understood only from the standpoint of their technical mastery and of their great sensual beauty. Their evocative power also derives from their literary content and especially from their inspiration from the classical myths of antiquity. Throughout Michael Ayrton's sculpture run tensions which correspond to the tug and pull between what could be called Daedalian inventiveness and Icarian destructiveness[12]. In many ways, these tensions symbolize those of twentieth century man, faced with an ever increasingly complicated and difficult world.

R. STANLEY JOHNSON
January   1984

NOTES

1 Quoted on page 28 of **Michael Ayrton** by Peter Cannon-Brookes.
2 From Michael Ayrton's introduction to the catalog of his Whitechapel Retrospective Exhibition.
3 Quoted on page 53 of Cannon-Brookes.
4 **Giovanni Pisano, Sculptor,** Thames and Hudson, London, 1970.
5 From : **Michael Ayrton : Drawings and Sculpture,** London, 1966.
6 Quoted on page 64 of Cannon-Brookes.
7 See page 102 of Ayrton's **The Maze Maker.**
8 Ayrton **The Maze Maker** page 68.
9 Quoted on page 113-114 of Cannon-Brookes.
10 Quoted on page 113 of Cannon-Brookes.
11 Page 282 of **The Maze Maker** by Michael Ayrton, London, 1967.
12 See : J.-E. Nyenhuis, introduction to : **Michael Ayrton : The Maze and Beyond,** Birmingham, Michigan, 1972.

DRAWINGS & PAINTINGS

SCULPTURE

BIOGRAPHIC NOTES

WORKS IN PUBLIC COLLECTIONS

BOOKS WRITTEN BY MICHAEL AYRTON

BOOKS ILLUSTRATED BY MICHAEL AYRTON

FILMS BY MICHAEL AYRTON

THEATRICAL PRODUCTIONS

BIBLIOGRAPHY

CATALOG

DRAWINGS & PAINTINGS

1. **Dark Trinity** (gouache), 1942.

2. **Figure with Flowering Laurel** (collage), 1962-64.

3. **Minotaur Enraged** (charcoal), 1963.

4. **Oracle with Crossed Feet** (black ink wash drawing), 1963

7. **Wheat Fragment** (acrylic and collage), 1965.

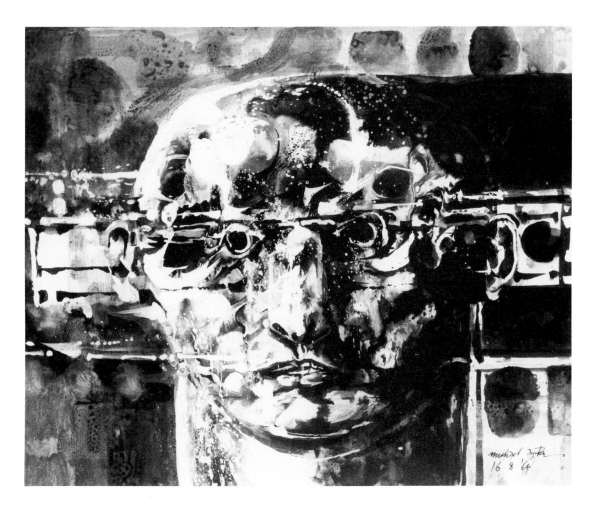

5. **Daedalus Mazemaker** (gouache and ink), 1964.

11. **Daedalus Head** (black ink wash), 1967.

12. **Shoreline, Crete** (collage with snakeskin), 1969.

10. **Maze Torso** (charcoal drawing on board), 1965.

13. **Extricator** (pen and ink wash and collage), 1969.

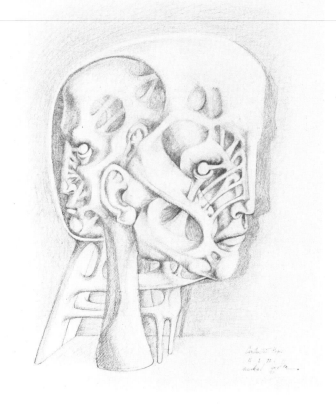

16. **Constructed Heads** (pencil drawing), 1972.

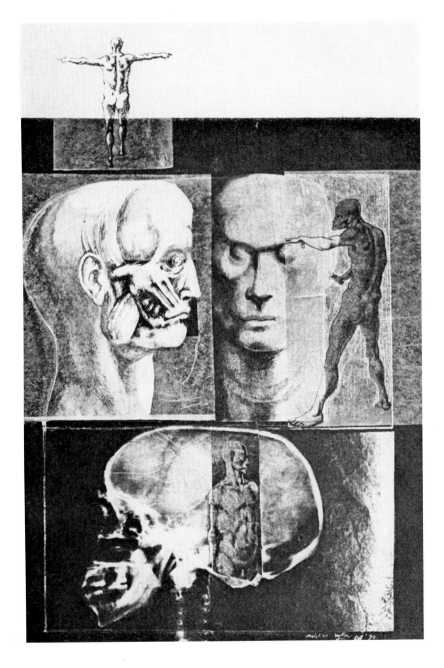

14. **Journey Through the Head** (ink, gouache and chalk drawing with collage), 1970.

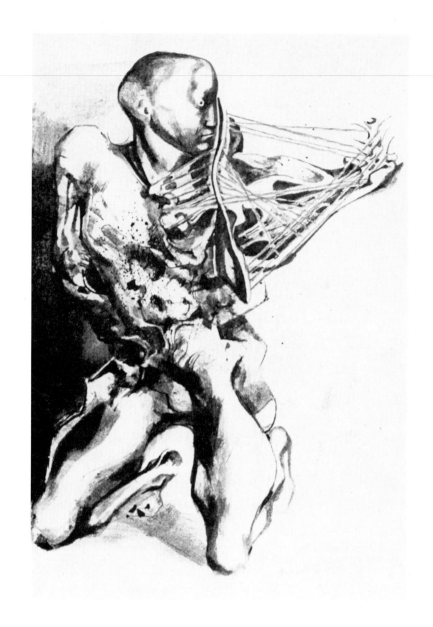

18. **Maze Music** (ink wash and red crayon over pencil), 1972.

17. **L'oiseau chante avec ses doigts -**
    The Bird Sings with His Fingers (ink and gouache drawing with collage), 1972.

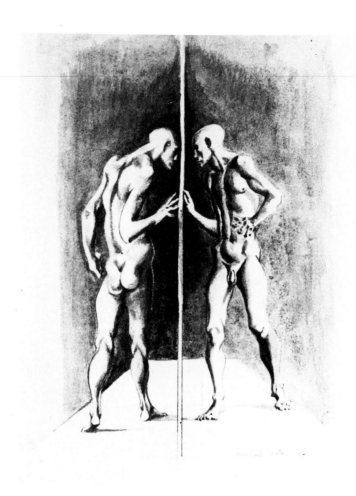

19. **Smoke Mirror Circle** (ink, wash and pencil drawing), 1972.

SCULPTURE

26. **Maze Torso** (bronze), 1955.

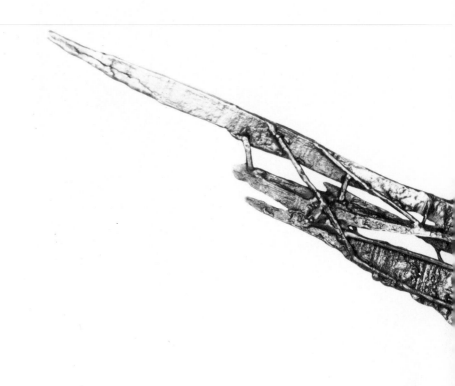

27. **Daedalus Wingmaker** (bronze), 1960.

29. **Oracle I** (bronze), 1962.

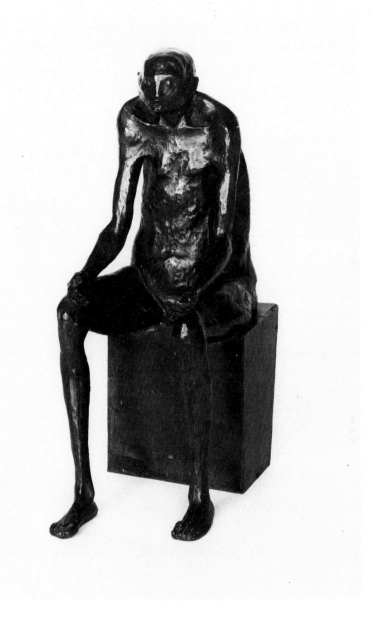

28. **Daedalus at Cumae** (bronze), 1961.

30. **Slender Sentinel** (bronze), 1962.

33. **Siren** (bronze), 1963.

36. **Maze Player** (bronze), 1965.

37. **Demeter Pregnant** (bronze), 1966.

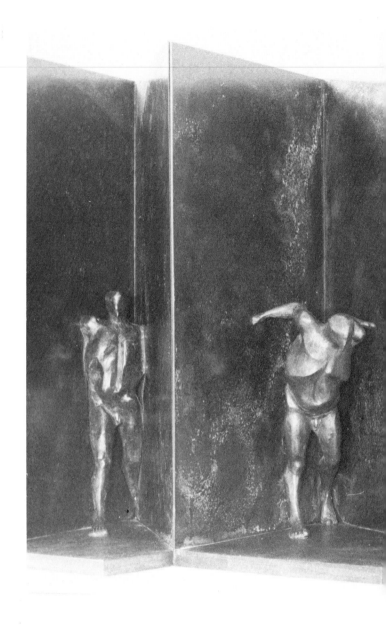

42. **Triptych II : Emerging Figure** (bronze), 1967.

43. **Minotaur Rising III** (bronze), 1968.

39. **Re-entry** (bronze), 1967.

45. **Reflex II** (bronze and perspex), 1969.

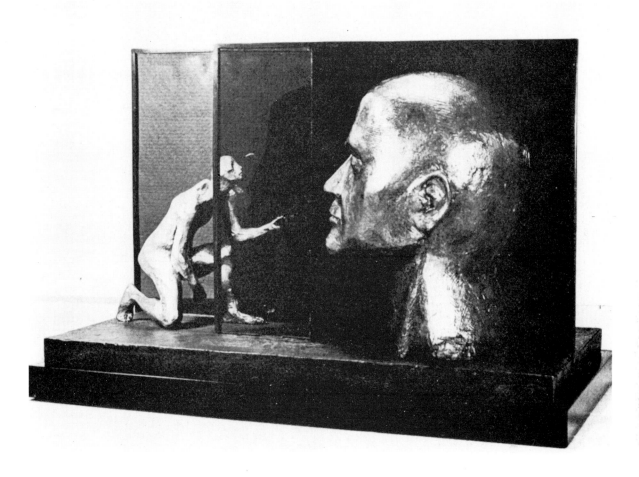

46. **Encounter** (bronze and perspex), 1969.

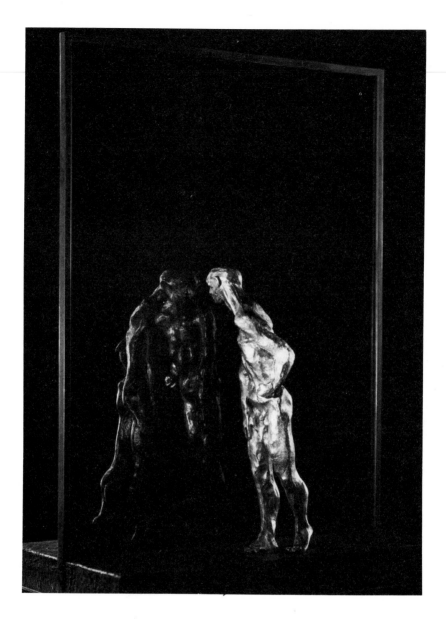

47. **Dioskouri** (bronze and perspex), 1970.

49. **Geode** (bronze and perspex), 1970.

50. **Minotaur Alarmed** (bronze), 1970.

51. **Sun Maze** (bronze), 1970.

Model of Ayrton sculpture and main entrance of the new S.S. Kresge Company International Headquarters building in Troy, Michigan.

THE S.S. KRESGE PROJECT

The new $ 26,000,000 corporate headquarters of the S. S. Kresge Company is designed to house an executive and administrative staff in excess of 2,500 persons. In this project, weathering steel and silo-size reddish-brown brick combine with reflective glass to form the exterior of the buildings. The whole area totals more than a half million square feet of floor space.

Michael Ayrton was selected as the artist for the main entrance courtyard sculpture. His successful model is in the vein of his recent «Reflector» series. Completed and put in place in October 1972, the sculpture stands 22 feets high and is constructed of cast bronze and reflective glass. The work rests on a bronze base. As envisioned by the sculptor, the sculpture consists of two abstract half-heads separated by a sheet of reflective glass. Each half-head is completed by its reflection. When viewed from the side, each head is fragmented by carved recesses into which are set other abstract head forms.

In commenting on this project, Ayrton states that : «The sculpture I shall make from these models for Kresge... will reflect the human head nine feet tall in a mirror fifteen feet high, but not only that, it will reflect a complex relationship of heads to one another. For while the highest and the most important factor that any of us comprehend is the human head, it is the conjunction of heads that human beings relate and combine to formulate concepts.»

53. **Reflective Head I** (bronze), 1971.

Smoke Mirror Circle (bronze and perspex), 1972.

55. **Figure with a Skein** (bronze), 1972.

60. **Troy Maze** (from the back : see opposite page), 1972.

60. **Troy Maze** (bronze and perspex), 1972.

64. **Mirror Twins** (bronze and perspex), 1973.

63. **Mirrored Figure II** (bronze and perspex), 1973.

65. **Cave** (bronze and perspex), 1974.

62. **Cord** (bronze, perspex and cord), 1973.

69. **Lens** (bronze and perspex), 1974.

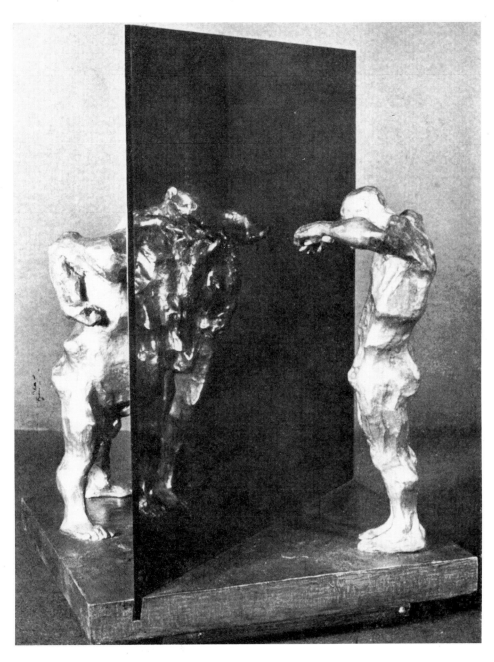

66. **Impact** (bronze and perspex), 1974.

70. **Reflection of Flight** (bronze and perspex), 1974-75.

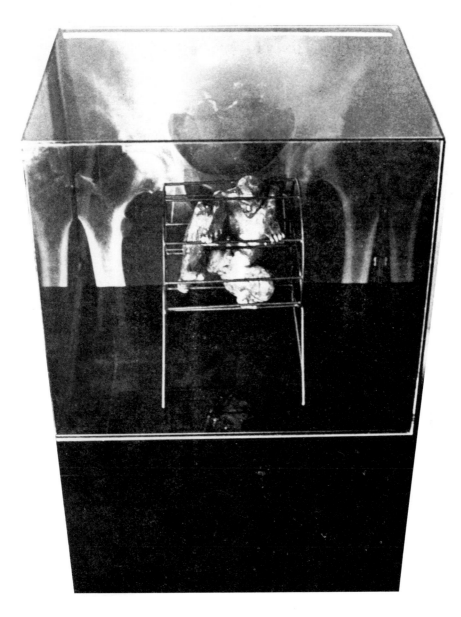

67. **Treadmill** (bronze and perspex), 1974.

71. **Minotaur Erect** (bronze), 1975.

BIOGRAPHIC NOTES

1921	Michael Ayrton was born in London, the son of Gerald Gould the poet, essayist, and literary critic, and Barbara Ayrton the socialist poltician who became Chairman of the Labour Party and M.P. for North Hendon.
1935	Leaves school, aged fourteen, to study at various art schools. Meets Henry Moore, Pavel Tchelitchev.
1936	Prolonged stay in Vienna, where he copies old masters in the Albertina Museum. Active in anti-Fascist movement related to the Spanish Civil War.
1937-39	Long periods in France. Shares Paris studio with John Minton.
1940	Begins to design «Macbeth» for John Gielgud, in collaboration with John Minton.
1941	Conscripted into the R.A.F. from which he is invalided out the following year.
1942	Joint exhibit with John Minton of paintings. Begins to teach life-drawing and theater design at the Camberwell School of Art.
1943	First one man exhibit in London.
1944	Becomes art critic for «The Spectator». Begins illustrating the first of some two dozen books. Designs scenery and costumes for the Sadler Wells Ballet production of «Le Festin de l'Araignée» with music by Albert Roussel. Meets Graham Sutherland, Paul Nash.
1945	Exhibit in London. Meets Wyndham Lewis.
1946	Collaboration with Constant Lambert on production of Purcell's «The Fairy Queen» for the Royal Opera House, Covent Garden. Publishes «British Drawings», Collins. First of yearly visits to Italy. Is influenced by painters of the early Renaissance, particularly Masaccio and Piero della Francesca. Exhibit of paintings in London.
1947	«Paintings by Michael Ayrton» published with introduction by James Laver. Travels extensively in Italy and France - painting, drawing and writing - from 1947 every year until 1952 and frequently thereafter. Discovers for himself the sculpture of Giovanni Pisano.
1948-50	Exhibits in London, Milano and Rome. Marries Elisabeth Balchin and acquires three stepdaughters.
1951-52	Makes films on drawings of Leonardo da Vinci. Exhibits in Cambridge, Zurich, London, Paris.
1953-54	Visits Spain. Exhibits in London and Stockholm. Begins to make sculpture. First visit to America.
1955	Retrospective exhibit (1945-55) of paintings, drawings, sculpture, book illustrations and theater designs at the Whitechapel Gallery in London and graphics exhibit in Berlin.
1956-57	Visits Cumae, near the Bay of Naples, and is inspired, for the first time, by the legend of Daedalus and Icarus. Publication of «Golden Sections», essays.
1958	Visits Greece for months as adviser to Basil Wright on making the film «The Immortal Land». During this time the landscape, myths and sculpture of Greece become his primary source of inspiration. Makes film, co-directed by Wright and Ayrton : «Greek Sculpture». Exhibits including Guggenheim Award Exhibition.
1959-62	Visits Mexico. Exhibits in England and the U.S.A. Publication of «The Testament of Daedalus called «The Maze Maker» was first published in England where it won the by C.P. Snow.
1963-68	Various group and individual exhibits in Nairobi, Philadelphia, London and Athens. Visits Sicily. Exhibits in Toronto, Oxford, Edinburgh, Chicago and others. His autobiography of Daedalus». Publication of «Drawings and Sculpture by Michael Ayrton» with introduction Heinemann Award for Literature.
1969	Bantam Books, New York edition of «The Maze Maker». Exhibits in London, Leeds, Edinburgh, other.
1970	Publication of «Giovanni Pisano, Sculptor» with an introduction by Henry Moore. Visits Cyprus. Completes «The Arkville Maze» (the largest labyrinth built since antiquity) for Armand G. Erpf's estate in the Catskill Mountains.
1971	Publication of «The Rudiments of Paradise». Various exhibits.
1972	Exhibition arranged by The National Book League in London : «Word and Image I & II : Wyndham Lewis and Michael Ayrton». Completion of the project for the main entrance of the new S.S. Kresge Compagny International Headquarters building in Troy, Michigan. 64 page catalog and Retrospective Exhibition of 76 works : «Michael Ayrton : The Maze : Bronzes, Drawings and Etchings from 1962-1972» at the R.S. Johnson-International Gallery, Chicago.

1973	Exhibits at the Portsmouth City Art Gallery, Southampton City Art Gallery, Holburne Museum, Bath, Exeter City Art Gallery, Rye Art Gallery. «Maze and Minotaur» retrospective organised by the Bruton Gallery. A very important retrospective organised by the University of Pennsylvania and also presented at the Haverford College in Pennsylvania. Bruton Gallery presents : «Ayrton : Works of the 1950's».
1975	Exhibit «Michael Ayrton : Recent Sculpture & Drawings 1972-1975» R.S. Johnson International, Chicago. On November 16, 1975, Michael Ayrton died of a heart attack in London.

* * *

1977	Various exhibits of the works of Michael Ayrton : Birmingham City Museums & Art Gallery ; Maplin Art Gallery, Sheffield ; Bradford Art Gallery and others under the title of : «The Compulsive Image : Sculpture, Paintings, Drawings, Reliefs and Theater Designs».
1978	One man exhibit at the Huntly Gallery, Canberra.
1979	Retrospective exhibition at the Darcy Gallery, Washington D.C.
1981	Scottish Arts Council retrospective at the Glasgow Aberdeen Collins Exhibition Hall and at the Edinburgh City Museum and Art Gallery. Another exhibition under the title of : «Recurring Themes and Images : Michael Ayrton» at the Bruton Gallery, Sommerset, National Museum of Wales and the Penarth Southwest Museum.
1984	Exhibit «Michael Ayrton : Retrospective Exhibition», 70 paintings, drawings and sculptures, R.S. Johnson International, Chicago.

31. **Small Sentinel** (bronze), 1962.

WORKS IN PUBLIC COLLECTIONS

GREAT BRITAIN

The Tate Gallery, London
The National Portrait Gallery, London
The Victoria and Albert Museum, London
The Arts Council of Great Britain
The British Council
The British Museum
City of London
The Art Gallery and Museum, Aberdeen
The Museum and Art Gallery, Birmingham
The City Art Gallery, Bristol
Fitzwilliam Museum, Cambridge
King's College, Cambridge
Pembroke College, Cambridge
St. Catherine's College, Cambridge
Trinity Hall, Cambridge
The Education Authority, Derby
The Museum and Art Gallery, Dudley
The RAF Museum, Hendon
The Ferens Gallery, Hull
The Museum and Art Gallery, Ipswich
The Education Authority, Leicester
The University of Liverpool
The City Art Gallery, Manchester
The Ashmolean, Oxford
Brasenose College, Oxford
Exeter College, Oxford
The City Art Gallery, Manchester
The Museum and Art Gallery, Reading
The Museum and Art Gallery, Salford
The City Art Gallery, Southampton
The Museum and Art Gallery, Southport
University, Exeter
The City Art Gallery, Exeter
The City Museum and Art Gallery, Stoke-on-Trent

The Museum and Art Gallery, Swindon
The City Art Gallery and Museum, Wakefield
The City Art Gallery, York
National Museum of Wales

UNITED STATES

The Museum of Fine Arts, Boston, Mass.
The Fogg Art Museum, Cambridge, Mass.
  (graphic collection)
The Art Institute, Chicago
Dartmouth University, Dartmouth, N.H.
The Art Institute, Detroit
The Wadsworth Atheneum, Hartford, Conn.
The Library of the Northwestern University, Evanston,
  Illinois
The Terre Haute Art Museum, Terre Haute, Ind.
The Museum of Modern Art, New York, N.Y.
  (graphic collection)
The Library of the U. of Texas
The Joslyn Art Museum, Omaha, Nebraska
The Museum of Art, Philadelphia, Penn.
National Air and Space Museum, Washington, DC

OTHER

Bibliotheque Nationale, Paris
The National Gallery of New South Wales, Sydney,
  Australia
The National Gallery of Canada, Ottawa, Canada
The Art Gallery of Ontario, Toronto, Canada
The Tel Aviv Museum, Tel Aviv, Israel
The Munitalp Foundation, Nairobi, Kenya

52. **Minotaur Risen** (bronze), 1971.

BOOKS WRITTEN BY MICHAEL AYRTON

BRITISH DRAWINGS	Collins, London	1946
HOGARTH'S DRAWINGS	Avalon Press, London	1948
TITTIVULUS, or THE VERBIAGE COLLECTOR	Max Reinhardt, London	1953
GOLDEN SECTIONS (essays)	Methuen, London	1957
THE TESTAMENT OF DAEDALUS	Methuen, London	1962
DRAWINGS AND SCULPTURE BY	Cory, Adams & McKay, London	1962
MICHAEL AYRTON	Revised edition	1966
THE MAZE MAKER	Longmans, Greene & Co., London	1967
	Holt, Rinehart & Winston, New York	1967
	Bantam Books, New York	1969
	Fischer Verlag, Frankfurt	1970
BERLIOZ, A SINGULAR OBSESSION	B.B.C. Publications, London	1970
GIOVANNI PISANO, SCULPTOR	Thames & Hudson, London	1970
	Weybright & Talley, N.Y.	1970
	Fischer Verlag, Frankfurt	1970
	Braun et Cie, Paris	1971
THE RUDIMENTS OF PARADISE (essays)	Secker & Warburg, London	1971
	Weybright & Talley, N.Y.	1971
FABRICATIONS	Becker & Warburg, London	1972
	Holt, Rinehart & Winston, N.Y.	1972
THE MIDAS CONSEQUENCE	Secker & Warburg, London	1974
	Doubleday, New York	1975

BOOKS ILLUSTRATED BY MICHAEL AYRTON

THE HIDDEN PATH **Frontispiece, pen drawing**	by David Cleghorn Thompson	Wm. Maclellan, Edinburgh, 1943
GILLES DE RAIS **4 line décorations**	Play by Cecil Gray	Favil Press, London, 1945
THE DUCHESS OF MALFI **10 litographs and 10 line drawings**	by John Webster	Sylvan Press, London, 1945
POEMS OF DEATH **16 4-colour lithographs**	chosen by Phoebe Poole	Adprint, London, 1945
CLAUSENTUM **7 wash drawings**	by John Arlott	Cape, London, 1946
THE BED **12 pen drawings**	by Cecil and Marjory Gray	Nicholson & Watson, London, 1946
IMPERIAL MISSION **9 pen drawings**	by Reinhold Schneider	Gresham Press, New York, 1948
POEMS OF JOHN KEATS **Frontispiece and line décorations**		Peter Nevill, London, 1958
THE UNFORTUNATE TRAVELLER **16 lithographs**	by Thomas Nashe	John Lehmann, London, 1948
THE UNFORTUNATE TRAVELLER **6 line drawings**	by Thomas Nashe	Capricorn Books, New York, 1960
THE PICTURE OF DORIAN GRAY **20 pen drawings**	by Oscar Wilde	Castle Press, London, 1948
MACBETH **8 4-colour lithographs**	by William Shakespeare	The Folio Society, London, 1951
MACBETH **8 theatre designs for John Gielgud's 1942 production by M. Ayrton and John Minton**	by William Shakespeare	The Folio Society, London, 1964
A SPELL FOR OLD BONES **16 pen drawings**	by Eric Linklater	P.A. Norsted, Stockholm, 1951
ENGLISH MYTHS AND LEGENDS **10 pen drawings**	by Henry Bett	B.T. Batsford Ltd., London, 1952
THE PENTAMERON **6 pen drawings**	by Gianbattista Basile	William Kimber, London, 1952
TITTIVULUS	by Michael Ayrton	Max Reinhart, London, 1953

60 lithographs		
GHOSTS AND WITCHES	by J. Wentworth Day	B.T. Batsford Ltd., London, 1954
20 pen drawings		
THE OTHER WING	by Louis Macneice	Aeriel Poems, Faber, London, 1954
1 4-colour lithograph		
2 pen drawings		
THE HUMAN AGE (2 vols.)	by Wyndham Lewis	Methuen, London, 1956 and 1957
9 monotypes, 2-colour monotype jackets		
TABLES OF MYSTERY AND IMAGINATION	by EA. Poe	The Folio Society, London, 1957
10 monotypes		
THE GOLDEN ASS	by Lucius Apuleus	The Folio Society, London, 1960
10 2-colour lithographs		
A DISTRACTION OF WITS	an anthology of Elizabethan verse, compiled by George Rylands	Cambridge University Press, 1958
12 2-colour line drawings		
NORTH OF ROME	by Richard Church	Hutchinson, London, 1960
7 line décorations		
THE ORESTEIA	by Aeschylus	The Limited Edition Club of New York, 1961
12 oil paintings in grisaille		
THE TESTAMENT OF DAEDALUS	by Michael Ayrton	Methuen, London, 1962
21 drawings and monotypes		
THREE PLAYS	by Euripides	The Limited Edition Club of New York, 1967
16 ink wash drawings		
THE MINOTAUR	by Michael Ayrton	Joseph Berkmann, London, 1970
13 pen, wash and charcoal drawings		
THE TRIAL AND DEATH OF SOCRATES	by Plato	Folio Society, London (in preparation)
8 pencil drawings		
THE EPIC OF GILGAMESH		The Limited Edition Cluf of New York (in preparation)

FILMS BY MICHAEL AYRTON

(in collaboration with Basil Wright)

THE DRAWINGS OF LEONARDO DA VINCI	The British Film Institue, London	1951
GREEK SCULPTURE	Marsden Films, London	1972
MAZE MAKER	Marsden Films, London	1972
THE DISCOVERY OF NAUTILUS	Being produced	

THEATRICAL PRODUCTIONS

(designed by Michael Ayrton)

MACBETH	By Wylliam Shakespeare, John Gielgud's production, London **(in collaboration with John Minton)**	1942
LE FESTIN DE L'ARAIGNEE	Ballet for the Sadlers Wells Co. Music by Albert Roussel. Choreography by Andrée Howard, London	1944
THE FAIRY QUEEN	Opera masque by Henry Purcell The Royal Opera House, Covent Garden Revived	1946 1951

BIBLIOGRAPHY

BASKIN, Leonard	A Note on Michael Ayrton	The Massachusetts Review, Vol. III, Nº 4, 1962
BLAKESTON, Oswald	A Profile of Michael Ayrton	Arts Review, Vol. XVIII, London, June 1966
BORGHESE, Leonardo	Catalogue Introduction	Galleria dell'Arte Obelisco, Rome, 1950
CAUSEY, Andrew	A Throng of Thoughts and Forms	Illustrated London News, June 4th, 1966
DAVIE, Donald	Michael Ayrton's «The Maze Maker»	The Southern Review, July 1969, Louisiana State University
DENVIR, Bernard	Michael Ayrton	Studio, London, March 1947
	Four Young English Painters	Graphis, Zurich, 1949
	Michael Ayrton	Arts News & Review, London, 1949
	«Daedalus Lives»	New York Review of Books, Nov. 23rd, 1967
GIELGUD, Sir John	Macbeth in Production	Theatre Arts Monthly, New York, 1942
HASKELL, Arnold	Ballet, 1939-45	The British Council, London, 1946
HENDY, Sir Philip	Michael Ayrton	Britain Today, London, 1949
	Catalogue Introduction	Wakefield City Art Gallery, 1949
	Catalogue Introduction	Galerie Galanis-Hentschel, Paris, 1953
HUGHES, Robert	Ayrton's Daedalus	Studio international, August, 1967
JOHNSON, R.Stanley	Michael Ayrton	Catalog introduction, exhibit at R.S. Johnson International, Chicago, 1972.
JOHNSON, R.Stanley	Michael Ayrton	Catalog introduction, exhibit at R.S. Johnson International, Chicago, 1975.
LAMBERT, Constant	Catalogue Introduction	Redfern international, London, 1945
	The face of Ischia, three paintings by Michael Ayrton	Lilliput, London, 1948
	Michael Ayrton as Theater Designer	Wakefield City Art Gallery, 1949
LAVER, James	Introduction to «Paintings by Michael Ayrton»	Grey Walls Press, London, 1947
LUCIE-SMITH, Edward	The Numinous in Modern Art	The Times, London, May 26th, 1964
LEWIS, Wyndham	Catalogue Introduction	Redfern Gallery, London, 1949
	A Note on Michael Ayrton's «Passion of the Vine»	«Nine», London, Summer 1950
	The Demon of Progress in the Arts	Methuen, London, 1954
	A Note on Michael Ayrton	Spectrum, Santa Barbara University, Vol. 1, Nº 2, 1957
	Introduction to «Golden Sections»	Methuen, London, 1957
MELVILLE, Robert	Michael Ayrton's «Temptation of St. Anthony»	Redfern Gallery, London, 1943
	A Panorama of Contemporary English Art	World Review, London, 1949
MIDDLETON, M.H.	Four English Romantics	Orpheus, John Lehmann, London, 1948
NYENHUIS, Jacob	«Daedalus and Icarus»	Graduate Comment, Wayne State University, Vol. X, Nº 4, 1967
PIPER, David	Catalog Introduction	The Magdalene Street Gallery, Cambridge
ORLANDO, Ruggiero	Michael Ayrton	Letteratura & Arte Contemporanea, Venice, 1951
READ, Sir Herbert	Contemporary British Art	Penguin Books, London, 1951 and 1964
	A Concise History of Modern Sculpture	Thames & Hudson, London, 1968
ROBERTSHAW, Ursula	Ayrton through the Labyrinth	Illustrated London News, 1972
ROBERTSON, Bryan	Catalogue Introduction	Whitechapel Gallery, London, 1955
	Michael Ayrton and the Theme of Icarus	Motif 7, London, 1951
	Ayrton's Work in Retrospect	The Times, London, June 24 th, 1969
ROSENTHAL, T.G.	Catalogue Introduction	Grosvenor Gallery, London, 1964
	Recent Work by Michael Ayrton	Studio International, London, 1966
	Catalog on Wyndham Lewis & Michael Ayrton	The National Book League, London, 1972

61. **Afternoon I** (bronze), 1973.

ROUVE, Pierre	**Michael Ayrton**	Arts Review, London, May 2nd, 1954
RYKWERT, Joseph	**La Scultura dit Michael Ayrton a Londra**	Domus, Milan, June 1967
SALT, Jim	**Michael Ayrton's Drawings, Catalogue Introduction**	University of Alberta, Canada, June 1965
SALVIAGGI, Guiseppe	**Disegni di Michael Ayrton**	Prospettiva Meridionale, Rome, 1960
SAVIDIS, George	**Catalogue Introduction**	Athens Hilton Gallery, 1964
SNOW, C.P.	**Introduction to «Michael Ayrton, Drawings and Sculpture»**	Cory, Adams & McKay, London, 1962 and 1966
SPENCER, Charles	**Michael Ayrton, Kai o Ikapoe**	Zygros, Athens, May 1962
STEINER, George	**Catalogue Introduction : Michael Ayrton, «A Debt to Hector Berlioz»**	Hamet Gallery, London, 1969
THOMPSON, Cynthia	**Michael Ayrton**	Time Magazine, July 9th, 1951
WARNER, Rex	**Introduction to «The Testament of Daedalus» by Michael Ayrton**	Methuen, London, 1962

68. **Sea Figure** (bronze), 1974.

20. **Mask II** (ink wash), 1974.

CATALOGUE

Paintings, Drawings, Etchings

1. **Dark Trinity** (from the St. Anthony series), 1942
   Gouache 16 x 13 inches
   Signed

2. **Figure with Flowering Laurel,** 1962-4
   Collage
   25.1/2 x 29 inches

3. **Minotaur Enraged,** 1963
   Charcoal
   25 x 16.1/2 inches
   Signed

4. **Oracle with Crossed Feet,** 1963
   Black Ink Wash
   20 x 14 inches
   Signed

5. **Daedalus Mazemaker,** 1964
   Gouache and Ink
   14 x 18 inches
   Signed

6. **Daedalus Head,** 1965
   Acrylic on Canvas
   11.1/2 x 15.1/2 inches
   Signed

7. **Wheat Fragment,** 1965
Acrylic & Collage
19 x 28 inches
Signed

8. **Demeter Head,** 1965
Black Ink Wash
15.1/2 x 19.1/2 inches
Signed

9. **Mazemaker,** 1965
White Chalk on Black Paper
18.1/2 x 24 inches
Signed

10. **Maze Torso,** 1965
Charcoal on Board
24 x 18 inches
Signed

11. **Daedalus Head,** 1967
Black Ink Wash
18.1/2 x 15 inches
Dated

12. **Shoreline, Crete,** 1969
Collage with Snakeskin
18.1/2 x 23.1/2 inches
Signed

13. **Extricator : Study for Bronze,** 1969
Pen & Ink Wash & Collage
15 x 19 inches
Signed

14. **Journey Through the Head,** October
1970.
Ink, Gouache & Chalk Drawing with
Collage
30 x 21.1/4 inches
Signed and dated lower right

15. **Maze Music,** 1972
Pencil
10 x 14 inches
Signed

16. **Constructed Heads,** 1972
Pencil
18.1/2 x 15 inches
Signed

17. **L'Oiseau chante avec ses doigts,**
March, 1972.
Ink & Gouache Drawing with Collage
30 x 21 inches
Signed and dated lower right

18. **Maze Music (Drawing I),** October 12,
1972
Ink Wash & Red Crayon over Pencil
20 x 13.1/4 inches
Signed, titled & dated lower right
On verso : A pencil drawing of the
head only.

19. **Smoke Mirror Circle,** October 30,
1972
Ink Wash & Pencil
18 x 12 inches
Signed, titled & dated lower right
On verso : A pencil drawing of a similar
figure from a different viewpoint.

20. **Mask II,** November 21, 1974.
Ink Wash
20 x 16 inches
Signed, titled & dated upper left.

21. **Study for Impact,** 1974
Black Ink Wash & Pencil
15 x 18.1/2 inches

22. **Cave I,** 1974
Black Ink Wash
14.1/2 x 11 inches
Signed

23. **Consecrated** (from the **Minotaur**
series), 1971
Etching
Edition of 75
13.1/2 x 21.3/8 inches
Signed & Numbered 14/75

24. **Rising** (from the **Minotaur** series), 1971
Etching
Edition of 75
15.5/8 x 21.1/2 inches
Signed & Numbered 14/75

25. **Revealed** (from the **Minotaur** series),
1971
Etching
Edition of 75
15.5/8 x 21.7/16 inches
Signed & Numbered 14/75

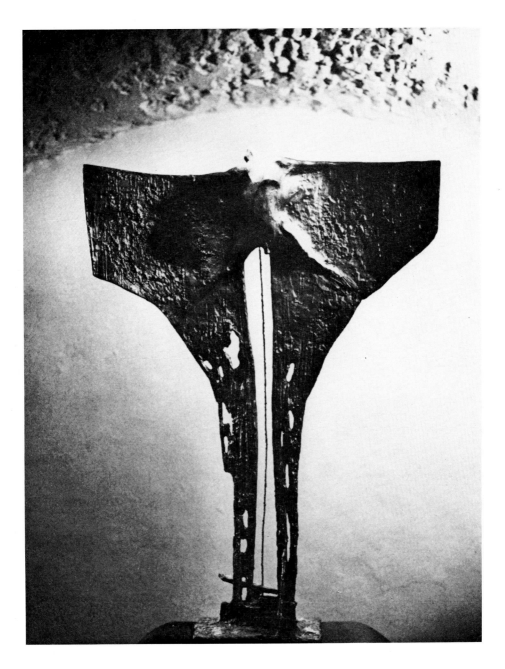

34. **Icarus Rišing Variant III** (bronze), 1965.

59. **Web (Cage Contingency)** (bronze and cord), 1972.

Bronzes

26. **Maze Torso**, 1955
Bronze
14.1/2 x 5.1/2 x 4.1/2 inches
Edition of

27. **Daedalus Wingmaker**, 1960
Bronze
18 x 22 x 15 inches
Edition of 6

28. **Daedalus at Cumae**, 1961
Bronze
21 x 11 x 7.1/2 inches
Edition of 6

29. **Oracle I**, 1962
Bronze
17 x 8.1/2 x 13 inches
Edition of 6

30. **Slender Sentinel**, 1962
Bronze
24 x 5.1/2 x 5.1/2 inches
Edition of 6

31. **Small Sentinel**, 1962
Bronze
9.1/2 x 5.1/2 x 5 inches
Edition of 12

32. **Fat Sentinel**, 1962
Bronze
18 x 5.1/2 x 5 inches
Edition of 9

33. **Siren**, 1963
Bronze
9.1/2 x 2.1/2 x 4 inches
Edition of 9

34. **Icarus Rising Variant III**, 1965
Bronze
30.1/2 x 23 x 8 inches
Edition of 9

35. **Mazemaker III**, 1965
Bronze
10 x 4.1/2 x 8 inches
Edition of 9

36. **Maze Player**, 1965
Bronze
15.1/2 x 12 x 15 inches
Edition of 9

37. **Demeter Pregnant**, 1966
Bronze
31 x 13 x 14 inches
Edition of 6

38. **Mirror Maze**, 1966
Bronze, Copper & Perspex
14 x 24 x 18.1/2 inches
Edition of

39. **Re-entry**, 1967
Bronze
23 x 21 x 17 inches
Edition of 9

40. **Waking Figures**, 1967
Bronze
5 x 15.1/2 x 11.1/2 inches
Edition of 9

41. **Triptych II (Emerging Figure)**, 1967
Bronze
14.3/4 x 16 x 12 inches
Edition of 9

42. **Triptych III (Emerging Figure)**, 1967
Bronze
37 x 50 x 18 inches
Edition of 9

43. **Minotaur Rising III**, 1968
Bronze
11.1/2 x 4 x 4 inches
Edition of 9

44. **Reflex I**, 1969
Bronze & Perspex
15.1/2 x 26 x 11 inches
Edition of 9

45. **Reflex II**, 1969
Bronze & Perspex
13 x 18.1/2 x 10 inches
Edition of 9

46. **Encounter**, 1969
Bronze & Perspex
14.3/4 x 15.1/2 x 26.1/2 inches
Edition of 9

47. **Dioskouroi**, 1970
Bronze & Perspex
19.1/2 x 14.1/2 x 8.1/2 inches
Edition of 9

48. **Extricator II**, 1970
Bronze
5.1/2 x 11 x 7.1/2 inches
Edition of 9

49. **Geode**, 1970
Bronze & Perspex
19.1/2 x 14.1/2 x 8.1/2 inches
Edition of 9

50. **Minotaur Alarmed**, 1970
Bronze
10 x 6 x 6 inches
Edition of 9

51. **Sun Maze**, 1970
Bronze
16.1/2 x 12 x 4 inches
Edition of 9

52. **Minotaur Risen**, 1971
Bronze
8.1/2 x 5 x 5.1/2 inches
Edition of 9

53. **Reflective Head I**, 1971
Bronze
21 x 14 x 9 inches
Edition of 9

54. **Reflective Head II**, 1971
Bronze
16 x 10 x 7 inches
Edition of 9

55. **Figure with a Skein**, 1972
Bronze
35 x 7.1/2 x 13 inches
Edition of 9

56. **Invader**, 1972
Bronze
16.1/2 x 21.1/2 x 8.1/2 inches
Edition of 12

57. **Maze Music**, 1972
Bronze & Cord
18 x 13 x 8.1/2 inches
Edition of 12

58. **Smoke Mirror Circle**, 1972
Bronze & Perspex
19.1/2 x 14.1/2 x 8.1/2 inches
Edition of 12

59. **Web (Cage Contingency)**, 1972
Bronze & Cord
69.1/2 x 13.1/2 x 10 inches
Edition of 9

59a. **Red Thread**, 1972
Bronze & Cord
7.1/2 x 12.1/2 x 3.1/2 inches
Edition of 12

60. **Troy Maze**
Bronze
29 x 48 x 18 inches
Edition of 9

61. **Afternoon I**, 1973
Bronze
4 x 5 x 5.1/2 inches
Edition of 12

62. **Cord**, 1973
Bronze, Perspex & Cord
18 x 14.1/2 x 8.1/2 inches
Edition of 12

63. **Mirrored Figure II**, 1973
Bronze & Perspex
15 x 8 x 5.1/2 inches
Edition of 12

64. **Mirror Twins**, 1973
Bronze & Perspex
16 x 9 x 8 inches
Edition of 12

56. **Invader** (bronze), 1972.

Ayrton sculpture in front of the S.S. Kresge Company International Headquarters in Troy, Michigan.

65. **Cave,** 1974
Bronze
15.1/2 x 18 x 15.1/2 inches
Edition of 12

66. **Impact,** 1974
Bronze
13 x 9.1/2 x 8.1/2 inches
Edition of 12

67. **Treadmill,** 1974
Bronze & Perspex
56.1/4 x 15.3/4 x 12 inches
Edition of 9

68. **Sea Figure,** 1974
Bronze
6 x 5 x 17.1/2 inches
Edition of 12

69. **Lens,** 1974
Bronze
12.1/4 x 14 x 8 inches
Edition of 9

70. **Reflection of Flight,** 1974-75
Bronze & Perspex
11.1/4 x 8.3/4 x 6 inches
Edition of 12

71. **Minotaur Erect,** 1975
Bronze
26 x 7 x 12 inches
Edition of 12

INDEX

Printed in France
IMP. LECERF
ROUEN